🎉 **Hey There, Awesome Reader!
Welcome to
"The BEST of Books"**

Where every page brings out the BEST in YOU!

✨ Imagination? Check!
💖 Kindness? You bet!
🦄 Adventures, giggles, and feel-good fun? All inside!

This series includes six illustrated storybooks and one super fun coloring book, all created to help YOU shine bright, dream big, and be your amazing self. Whether you're reading a story or coloring your own, there's no wrong way to play.
Your way is the BEST way!
So, grab your favorite book, flip the page,
and let your BEST shine through!

🌟 Explore the full series at:

(www.TheBESTOfBooks.com)

THE BEST OF series

THE BEST OF
Christmas

written by J R PHILP

art by Chris Padovano

All Books In The BEST of Series. . . by J R Philp

- The BEST of America
- The BEST of Christmas
- The BEST of Life Vol. 1
- The BEST of All of Us Vol. 2
- The BEST of Fun Vol. 3
- The BEST of Colors and Shapes Vol. 4
- My Coloring Book is The BEST

Copyright © 2018 by J R Philp
All rights reserved.

No part of this publication may be reproduced, stored in a retrieval system, or transmitted in any form or by any means - electronic, mechanical, photocopying, recording, or otherwise - without the prior written permission of the publisher, except in the case of brief quotations used in reviews or articles.

For information regarding bulk purchases, educational use, or special editions, please contact the publisher at: info@seibroinc.com

This book is a work of original authorship.
Story by J R Philp | Illustrated by Chris Padovano
Layout, design, and typography by Seibro Inc
Published by Seibro Inc
Tampa, FL

Printed in the United States of America
First Edition, 2018

TheBestofBooks.com

10 9 8 7 6 5 4 3 2 1

The Christmas Angel on top of the tree is the BEST!

Frosty the Snowman is the BEST! I love him

My mom's Christmas cookies are the BEST!

My Christmas stocking is the BEST! I can't wait to see the surprises.

Making a gingerbread house with mom is the BEST!

My mom and dad reading "The Night Before Christmas" is the BEST!

My mittens and scarf are the BEST!

Christmas cards are the BEST!

Santa's reindeer are the BEST!

Do you know their names?

Santa's elves are the BEST.
They work so hard.

The first snow fall is the BEST!

and a sunshine Christmas is also the BEST!

Waiting for Santa is the BEST!

Ice Skating on a frozen lake is the BEST!

Giving gifts to others is the BEST!

🎈 About The BEST of Books Series

Get ready to dream big, think kind thoughts, and smile from the inside out!
Each book in "The BEST of Books" series celebrates the little things that make life magical, like a giggle, a good idea, or a splash of color. Whether you're reading with a friend or coloring on your own, these stories remind us that the BEST moments are often the simplest ones.

✨ Collect them all and share the joy:

- ❖ "The BEST of Christmas"
- ❖ "The BEST of America"
- ❖ "The BEST of Life"
- ❖ "The BEST of All of Us"
- ❖ "The BEST of Colors and Shapes"
- ❖ "The BEST of Fun"
- ❖ "My Coloring Book Is The BEST"

📚 Keep exploring at:
www.TheBESTOfBooks.com